For Levi, there's always a great word waiting to be illustrated.
— R.V.

For Spence and Evie, keep your torches on wherever you go.
—J.B.

First published 2021

EK Books
an imprint of Exisle Publishing Pty Ltd
PO Box 864, Chatswood, NSW 2057, Australia
226 High Street, Dunedin, 9016, New Zealand
www.ekbooks.org

A CiP record for this book is available from the National
Library of Australia.

ISBN 978-1-925820-84-3

Designed by Joanna Bartel
Typeset in Filson Soft and Baskerville.
Printed in China

This book uses paper sourced under ISO 14001 guidelines
from well-managed forests and other controlled sources.

10 9 8 7 6 5 4 3

THE art of WordS

Robert Vescio · Joanna Bartel

EK

They are found
in between the pages
of this book!

THERE.

Some words are

BIG.

Some words are

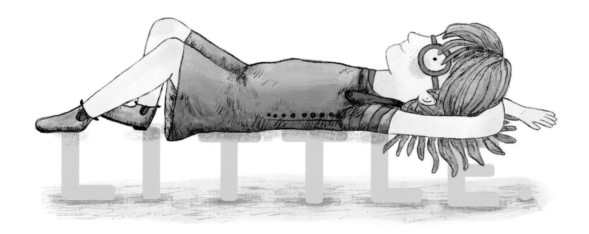

Others are COLOURFUL.

Some are

They can be  **SHORT**ENED.

They can be

EXTE

A few **wow** in reverse...

or Simply Trust And Never Doubt for something else.

Sometimes they need a friend:

a **?** for words that **ask**,

a **,** for words that **pause** or **list**,

an  for words that sh**out**,

and a for words that end or abbreviate.

They are fun to

Many are BRILLIANT...

or **PLAIN.**

But best of all ...

WORDS
string
TOGETHER
like droplets of dew
on a silky web...

and
SHAPE
the
HEART
with happiness
through stories...